DK Eye Wonder

Big Cats

LONDON, NEW YORK, MUNICH,
MELBOURNE, and DELHI

Written and edited by Sarah Walker
Designed by Jacqueline Gooden
Managing editor Sue Leonard
Managing art editor Rachael Foster
US editors Margaret Parrish and Gary Werner
Jacket design Chris Drew
Picture researcher Sarah Pownall
Production Kate Oliver
DTP designer Almudena Díaz
Consultant Derek Lyon

First American Edition 2002

04 05 06 07 08 09 10 9 8 7 6

Published in the United States by
DK Publishing, Inc.
375 Hudson Street
New York, NY 10014

DK publishing offers special discounts for bulk purchases for sales promotions or premiums.
Specific, large-quantity needs can be met with special editions, including
personalized covers, excerpts of existing guides, and corporate imprints.
For more information, contact Special Markets Department, DK Publishing Inc.,
95 Madison Avenue, New York, NY 10016 Fax: 800-600-9098.

Walker, Sarah.
Big cats / by Sarah Walker. -- 1st American ed.
p.cm. -- (Eye Wonder)
Summary: A simple presentation of the physical characteristics, habitat,
and life cycle of such big cats as the leopard, tiger and puma.
ISBN 0-7894-8548-6 -- ISBN 0-7894-8549-4
1. Felidae--Juvenile literature [1. Felidae. 2. Cats.] I. Title. II. Series.
QL737.C23 W33 2001
599.75'5--dc21

Color reproduction by Colourscan, Singapore
Printed and bound in Italy by L.E.G.O.

see our complete
product line at
www.dk.com

Contents

Introducing cats

Fossils show that catlike creatures have existed for many millions of years. All cats belong to the same family group called the *Felidae*. In size order, the seven biggest cats in the world are the tiger, lion, jaguar, leopard, snow leopard, puma, and the cheetah.

The largest cat in the world is the Amur tiger. It can be up to 13 ft (4 m) long, from head to tail.

Domestic cats are popular pets.

The bobcat is one of the smaller cats.

Ancient ancestor

Smilodon, a huge, saber-toothed cat, lived in open grasslands about 11,000 years ago. Fossil evidence shows that it lived in family groups, similar to modern-day lions.

The tiger is the most powerful cat in the world.

Top of the ladder

Big cats are at the top of the hunting pyramid, which means there are few of them compared to other animals. Big cats can be very tall; their height is measured from their shoulder to the tips of their paws.

The puma is a purring cat!

How tall are you compared to these cats?

3 ft 9 in (120 cm)

3 ft 3 in (100 cm)

2 ft 5 in (75 cm)

1ft 8in (50 cm)

10 in (25 cm)

0 cm

5

Cat habitats

There are 37 species of wild cat in the world. From snow-capped mountains to deserts, and grasslands to tropical rain forests, cats of all shapes and sizes roam the Earth.

Cats around the world

The map below shows where the seven biggest cat species live. Most are found between the tropics of Cancer and Capricorn, where the weather is warm all year round, and where there are wet and dry seasons.

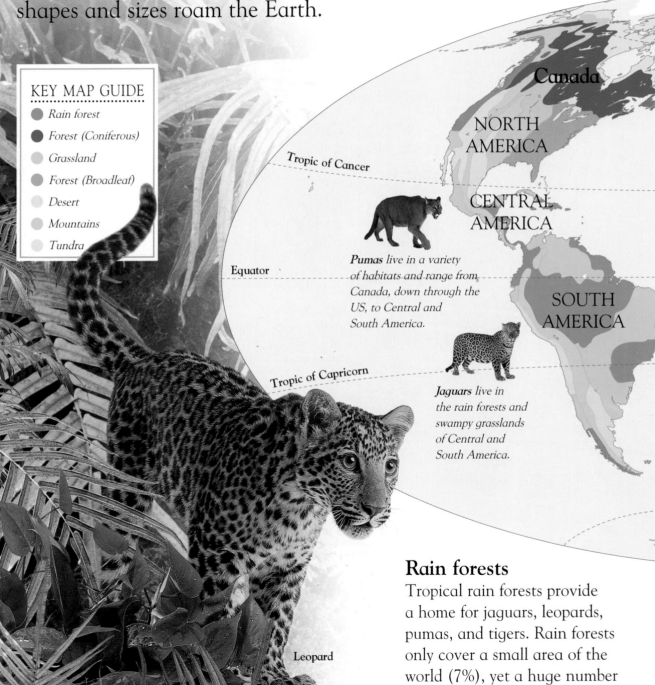

KEY MAP GUIDE

- Rain forest
- Forest (Coniferous)
- Grassland
- Forest (Broadleaf)
- Desert
- Mountains
- Tundra

Tropic of Cancer

Equator

Tropic of Capricorn

Canada

NORTH AMERICA

CENTRAL AMERICA

SOUTH AMERICA

Pumas live in a variety of habitats and range from Canada, down through the US, to Central and South America.

Jaguars live in the rain forests and swampy grasslands of Central and South America.

Leopard

Rain forests

Tropical rain forests provide a home for jaguars, leopards, pumas, and tigers. Rain forests only cover a small area of the world (7%), yet a huge number of animals live in them.

An icy home

Few cats live in harsh mountain areas. Only the snow leopard lives high up in the freezing Asian mountains.

Russian Federation

Siberia

EUROPE

China

ASIA

India

AFRICA

Snow leopards live in the mountains of central Asia.

Leopards live in the forests and grasslands of Africa as well as parts of Asia.

Southeast Asia

Tigers live in the forests of India, Siberia and Southeast Asia.

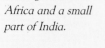

Lions live in prides in the grasslands of Africa and a small part of India.

Cheetahs live in the grasslands of Asia as well as southern and eastern Africa.

AUSTRALIA

ANTARCTICA

Glorious grasslands

The rich grasslands of Africa are home to several of the big cats. During the wet season the land is green and partially flooded, yet barren in the dry season.

Inside and out

Designed to be superb hunters, big cats are a strong species. A fur coat covers a tough skeleton, which protects the internal body parts. Powerful muscles allow each cat to move with great flexibility and agility.

Vertebrae of the spine

Rib cage

Bare bones
All cats have very similar skeletons, with a large cranium (brain case), strong back legs, a deep rib cage, and a flexible spine. The length of a cat's tail varies between animals.

Fantastic fur
A fur coat protects cats from the weather and helps to camouflage them. It also allows them to transfer their scent. All wild cats have two layers of fur. Only the top coat is patterned.

Long tailbone

Back leg bone

A supple spine
Cheetahs are the fastest land animals in the world. These pictures show that the cat's spine flexes and extends as it runs. This increases the length of the stride, allowing distances to be covered very quickly.

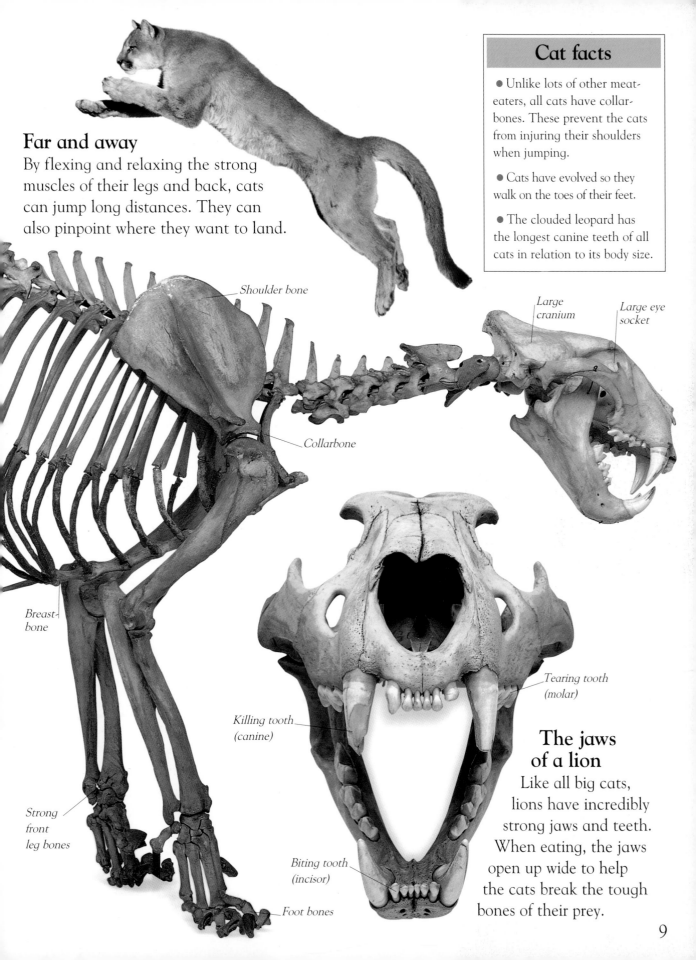

Far and away
By flexing and relaxing the strong muscles of their legs and back, cats can jump long distances. They can also pinpoint where they want to land.

Shoulder bone

Large cranium

Large eye socket

Collarbone

Breast-bone

Tearing tooth (molar)

Killing tooth (canine)

The jaws of a lion
Like all big cats, lions have incredibly strong jaws and teeth. When eating, the jaws open up wide to help the cats break the tough bones of their prey.

Strong front leg bones

Biting tooth (incisor)

Foot bones

9

A cat's life

All cats, big or small, spend their time engaged in the same sort of activities. Hunting, eating, sleeping, cleaning, and playing are all regular events in the lives of cats.

Clean cats

Cats are very clean creatures and spend a lot of time grooming. Members of the same cat family often wash each other to strengthen bonds and spread their scents around.

Licking helps to keep cats cool in hot temperatures.

This leopard's rough tongue is used as a comb for cleaning.

Cat napping

Cats are officially the sleepiest animals in the world, spending about two-thirds of their lives asleep. This is a great way of saving energy, which they need for hunting.

Even when fast asleep, cats' senses remain alert.

All cats spend about 19–20 hours of the day resting.

Burst of energy

Cats hunt to survive, and this uses up a lot of energy. Generally, cats hunt in similar ways, slowly stalking, then quickly and expertly ambushing their prey. A hunt may or may not be successful!

Supersenses

Most cats hunt alone and at night so they constantly rely on their highly tuned supersenses. Sight, smell, hearing, taste, and touch are all much more highly developed in cats than in humans.

Sound

Large, funnel-shaped ears draw sound into them. Cats' can hear even the smallest of noises, which helps them to detect potential prey.

Sight

Cats have excellent eyesight and can see up to six times better than humans in dim light.

A special sense

Cats have a special organ in the roof of their mouths, called the Jacobson's organ. This allows them to "taste" smells. When the cat curls back its lips (a process known as "flehming"), it can analyze scents that other cats have left behind.

Bright eyes

Cats are known for their brilliant eyesight, and eyes that glow in the darkness. When it is dark, cats' pupils expand to let in lots of light so the cats can see. The pupils then narrow again when it is brighter.

Narrow pupils in the light.

Expanded pupils in the dark.

Touch

Whiskers are long, stiff hairs with nerve endings at the roots. Framing the cat's face, these hairs help it to feel its way around, by providing the cat with information about its environment.

Smell

A sensitive nose helps each cat to recognize its home, mate, family, and food. A cat's nose has about 19 million nerve endings in it.

Taste

A large, rough tongue is used for grooming, licking meat from bones, and lapping up water.

SENSITIVE SENSES

All cats are extremely sensitive to vibrations in the air. Some may even sense earthquake tremors and volcano eruptions before they occur. People living on the slopes of Mount Etna, an active volcano in Italy, often keep pet cats as early warning devices. When the cats run away in terror, their owners quickly follow!

Run!

Cat comparisons

The whole feline family shares certain physical features and characteristics. A pet cat creeping up on its prey in the yard behaves in a very similar way to a big cat stalking and hunting its prey in the wild.

Treetop rest
Cats have the ability to perch in the most difficult places. A long tail helps the animals to balance, and paws are spread out to support weight. All young cats have to learn to climb, and usually have a few accidents along the way!

Fit as a feline

Cats don't need to exercise to stay in shape. When they stretch and roll, their muscles receive a thorough workout.

Cat facts

- A cat's tail clearly shows what mood it is in. It will be lashed around when angry, or raised high when greeting or exploring new places.

- Cats swallow their food without chewing, as they don't have any grinding teeth.

On the prowl

All cats have a strong hunting instinct, and wild cats must kill in order to survive. Well-fed domestic cats have food provided, but the urge to hunt is not easily forgotten.

Cat calls

The leopard is one of the four roaring cats, along with the tiger, lion, and jaguar. The other big cats can growl and make chirping noises. Cats' noises communicate their feelings, and meowing, purring, growling, or roaring indicate a wide range of emotions.

King of the beasts

African lions are found on the grassy plains of southern and eastern Africa, living in groups called prides. Prides can have as few as five lions in them, or as many as 40. With its crowning mane and regal looks, the male lion is often associated with royalty.

Male lions are so big that it is difficult for them to hunt.

Land of the lion
One of the male lion's roles is to protect his pride and territory from rival males. Each dawn he roars loudly, announcing to the world that it is his kingdom, so intruders beware!

Daytime dozers

Lions are at their most active at night, when the
sun has set and the temperature is cooler. In the
heat of the day they spend most of their time
resting and sleeping in the shade, only waking
up for a quick drink or to play.

Extended family

The pride consists of related females and
only a few males. Lionesses hunt to feed
the group, as well as take care of the cubs.

Cat facts

- Lions can live for up to
15 years in the wild.

- There are more African
lions than Asiatic lions,
which can only be found in
a very small area of India.

- A lion's roar can be heard
up to 5 miles (8 km) away.

- The lion's mane makes him
look bigger then he actually is,
and protects his throat from the
claws and teeth of other males.

Tiger tales

Tigers are the largest and most powerful of all the big cats. A tiger is 10 times stronger than a man. All five types of tiger are covered in dazzling stripes, and each animal's markings are unique, just like human fingerprints.

The biggest of them all

Living in the freezing woodlands of eastern Russia, China, and North Korea, Amur tigers are the largest of all tigers. A thick, furry coat protects them from the cold.

A rare sight

Only Bengal tigers give birth to white cubs, and these are very rare. Few white tigers exist in the wild.

Skills for life

These cubs may be playing a fun game, but play fights will teach them vital skills. When they are older they will have to fend for themselves, and protect their own territories and cubs.

Fun in the water
Although they spend most of their time on land, tigers do love the water. They often lounge around in the water to cool down in the heat of the day.

Water cat

The third largest of all the big cats, the jaguar lives in areas of Central and South America. Found in swampy grasslands and dense tropical rain forests, it lives and hunts in the water as well as on the ground.

Strong swimmers

Jaguars love swimming. They are never far from the water and regularly patrol the riverbanks looking for food.

What's for dinner?

Jaguars have a varied diet, ranging from lizards and fish, to birds and small alligators! Fish are one of their favorite dishes – jaguars simply flip them out of the water with their huge paws. Jaguars' incredibly strong jaws easily pierce the skulls of their larger victims.

Black beauty

Black jaguars also have spotted markings, although it can be difficult to see these on their dark coats. These black cats can appear with "normal" jaguars in mixed litters of cubs.

A jaguar has the most powerful jaws and teeth of all cats.

These rosettes are larger than a leopard's and have a dark marking at the center.

THE WARRIOR CAT

The jaguar is a common symbol of strength and power in South America, and is linked with royalty and bravery. In Mayan civilization, the jaguar was thought to protect and guard the royal family.

Speed king

The cheetah is unusual compared to the other big cats, which have large, sturdy bodies. Built for speed and agility, the cheetah has a small head, a long, streamlined body, and thin, powerful legs. Swift and slender, it is the fastest land animal in the world.

A crying cat

The distinctive black stripes on a cheetah's face are often referred to as tear stripes. It is possible that these help to reduce the glare of the sun.

Can't catch me!

The cheetah can reach its maximum speed of about 112 kph (70 mph) in under three seconds. This is faster than a sports car can accelerate. Not surprisingly, it can only keep up this pace for a few minutes.

CHEETAH TRAINING

Although it seems odd now, in the 16th century cheetahs were often caught when young and trained to help huntsmen kill antelope and gazelle. Cheetahs' were sent after prey and, after knocking the animal down, would wait for their owners to complete the kill and remove the body.

Watchful cheetah

Cheetahs tend to have large territories. They need to keep a constant watch over their area, as competition for food and space is fierce.

Due to its build and speed, the cheetah is often compared to the greyhound.

Motherly love

To prevent the cubs from being killed by predators when they are young, the mother moves them to new locations on a daily basis. The cubs are covered in spiked fur when they are small, this camouflages them in the grass, and makes them look bigger.

Head for heights

To a leopard, a tall tree with plenty of branches is the perfect place to have a nap and observe the land. Dozing throughout the day, they are active at night.

Cat facts

• Black leopards are called panthers.

• A leopard's whiskers are extremely long. These help the cats to find their way around when they are high up in a tree.

• Clouded leopards are sometimes spotted hanging from tree branches by their back legs.

Lounging leopards

Leopards are one of the most easily recognizable big cats, with their distinctive spots, long tail, and treetop activities. They make their homes in a variety of habitats, from mountain heights to tropical rain forests.

There's mom

Each leopard has a white tip on the end of its tail. The young cubs follow this tip when they are learning to hunt.

Leopards often come down from the trees to bask in the sunshine.

Dinner in a tree

This cunning cat eats a variety of animals, ranging from insects to giraffe calves. Leopards often store their food in the branches of a tree, away from other predators. Here they can eat when they like!

These markings look like clouds, hence the name given to the clouded leopard.

Clouded cousin

The clouded leopard is a different species from "normal" leopards. It is much smaller and very rare. It also loves climbing trees.

Powerful pumas

There are several species of puma, all of which live in parts of North and South America. Muscular and athletic, pumas are fast movers, good swimmers, and excellent climbers. They avoid contact with humans and are rarely seen.

Pumas are fantastic at the long jump, managing huge leaps of about 40 ft (12 m).

On the prowl
Pumas have different territories during the winter and summer, which they migrate to and from each year. Male pumas have larger territories than female pumas.

Hot and cold
Varying climates are not a problem for these tough cats – they can cope with snowy mountains, tropical forests, and scorching, hot scrublands.

Small beginnings
Puma cubs are born with bright blue eyes and spotted fur. These fade when they are a few months old. The cubs are blind and deaf until they are three weeks old.

Feline in flight
Being able to jump so far is a very useful skill to have, as pumas spend a lot of time running and leaping over rocky ground. They can also leap onto the back of their prey when they are hunting!

CAT OF MANY NAMES
Confusingly, pumas are called a variety of names. Cougar, mountain lion, panther, red tiger, Mexican lion, silver lion, and catamount are all names used to describe them!

Snow cat

Living high up in the icy mountains of Central Asia, little is known about the shy and solitary snow leopard. These beautiful cats are rarely spotted by humans, as they live in large, isolated areas.

Happy families

Snow leopards have their babies in the spring. The cubs stay with their mother through their first winter, before leaving to find homes of their own.

A snow leopard's tail can be up to 35 in (90 cm) long.

The traveling cat

Each snow leopard has a huge territory, which it will patrol regularly. Every cat has to travel a long way to find suitable prey, such as wild sheep and goats.

Cat facts

● Snow leopards live about 9,800 ft (3000 m) up in the mountains.

● Although they cannot roar, snow leopards do make a high-pitched yowling noise.

● There are only about 4,000 snow leopards left in the world. They are often killed for their distinctive fur coat.

A thick fur coat protects the cat from freezing temperatures.

Large paws act as snow shoes.

Balancing act

The snow leopard's mountainous domain means that each cat spends a lot of time climbing and balancing. Short and powerful limbs, strong chest muscles, and cushioned furry paws make the snow leopard an agile rock climber.

Team tactics

Living in their family groups, lions are the only big cats to regularly hunt as a team. Lionesses are the hard workers, using their combined group strength and tactics to catch and kill prey.

Prowling predator
This lioness is stalking prey. Her body is right next to the ground and her ears and tail are down. Padded paws allow her to creep along silently.

The winning team

Working as a team to bring down this unfortunate wildebeest, these lionesses will soon finish the kill. However, an animal this size won't provide a lot of food for a large pride.

Although not helping with the kill, this lioness will share the meal.

Gripping the animal by its throat, the lioness will quickly suffocate it.

Food for all?

When the kill is complete, the lions begin to feed. Although rightfully the female hunters should eat first, it is normally the males who get the best parts. They may even steal the meat from the females, then share it with the cubs!

Solitary killers

All big cats are meat eaters and need to hunt successfully in order to survive. Most cats hunt alone, and each species has its own method of catching prey, including running, leaping, and even climbing trees!

High-speed chase

Incredibly fast and well-balanced when running, the cheetah moves and sways in perfect time with the movements of its prey.

A long tail acts as a rudder to help the cheetah balance.

Jump for your dinner

Servals hunt a variety of animals, and this low-flying bird makes a tasty feast. These agile, medium-sized cats can leap almost 10 ft (3 m) into the air.

Nowhere to run to

Pumas are excellent tree-climbers, so it is unlikely that this raccoon will escape to safety. If a puma cannot finish its meal, it will cover it up with leaves and shrubs and return to it at a later time.

Life on the plains

Some cats make their homes in grasslands, plains, and even deserts. These animals need to be tough to cope with barren surroundings, and are usually active at night when the temperatures are cooler.

Curious cat

With their oversized ears and long legs, servals look like no other cat! Living in the grasslands and savannas of Africa, a serval's long legs allow it to bound through the tall grasses.

Large ears help the serval to detect prey far away.

High flyer

Caracals are found in the scrublands of
Africa and the dry and rocky parts of Asia.
Agile and stealthy, caracals often leap
high up into the air to catch birds,
but also eat rodents and other small
creatures. Their amazing tufted ears
are very sensitive to sounds, and, as
with some other cats, also indicate
the cat's mood and intentions.

Last of the lynxes

These rare, heavily spotted
Spanish lynxes are found mostly
in southwestern Spain. They
eat mainly rabbits but, like
the caracal and the serval,
sometimes catch low-flying birds.

35

Forest felines

Lots of the smaller wild cats make their homes in a variety of forest environments, from woodlands to rain forests. These woody homes provide the cats with lots of space and shelter, and contain plenty of food.

A forest lynx
The European lynx is found in northern Asia, and is being reintroduced back into woody parts of Europe. This sturdy cat hardly ever runs, although it will walk a long way in search of food.

This cat's short fur dries off quickly when it has finished fishing.

Fishing forest cat

The curious fishing cat isn't afraid of getting wet. Making its home in the thickly planted areas around swamps and rivers, slightly webbed feet help this feline to bat a fishy feast out of the water.

Different colored cats

Each ocelot has individual markings, and their coats can range from a rich yellow and cream to a dark brown. Active at night, this medium-sized cat likes to spend its days curled up in the safety of a tree.

American beauty

The bobcat is America's most common native cat. A small species of lynx, it is active day and night, and is known to pounce on prey from the trees.

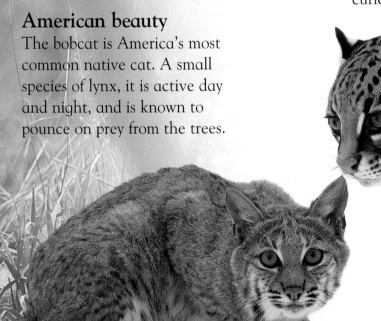

Cat families

Nearly all cats are solitary creatures. Although cat mothers raise their cubs carefully, most return to the single life when their young can take care of themselves. Lions are the only cats to live in permanent family groups.

Pride of the family
A pride of lions is made up of a group of related females and their young. Several females may give birth at similar times and produce milk for each others' cubs, as well as rearing their young families together.

Cub carriage

All mother cats can carry their young with their mouths. By grasping the loose skin around the cub's neck, the mother can carry the cub without hurting it.

The cub completely relaxes in its mother's mouth.

Safe with mom

Pumas give birth to between one and six cubs, after a pregnancy of about three months. The cubs drink their mother's milk until they are two or three months old.

Cat facts

- Male lions do live in prides, but are always heavily outnumbered by lionesses!

- Many cats give birth to their cubs in dens. Here they are raised safely, out of harms' way.

- Puma siblings may stay together for a while, even after they have left their mother.

Undercover cats

All big cats need to be able to blend in with their environment. This helps them to hunt successfully, and to hide from possible dangers. It is often very hard to see cats in the wild, as spots, stripes, and rosettes help them melt into the background.

A nice place for a rest
A leopard's spots and golden fur prove an effective camouflage when hunting, prowling, and sleeping in the plains and grasses.

Forest disguise

The dark rosettes, golden fur, and white underbelly of the jaguar mean it blends in perfectly with the dappled light of the forest. It could be a nasty surprise for any unsuspecting, passing prey!

Is it a branch. . .

. . .or a lynx?! This medium-sized cat has a tawny and cream-colored coat, perfect for hiding in a tree. A strong climber, it surveys its territory from the safety of a branch.

All cats can stay still
for long periods of time,
making them hard to spot.

Night stalkers

Most big cats are active at dawn, dusk, and at night. Cats prefer to hunt under the cover of darkness, and their highly-tuned senses make them very successful night-time predators.

Calm in the storm

These lionesses are relaxed, despite the storm behind them. Although always part of a pride, individuals do drift off into smaller groups at times. At dusk the females awake from a day's dozing and begin to hunt.

Midnight feast

Leopards become active when the sun goes down and the temperatures are cooler. This cat has just caught an impala, which was ambushed under the cover of darkness.

A stroll in the dark

This tiger's striped markings are a striking sight in the darkness. Tigers may walk vast distances in one night in the search for prey, prowling silently through the forests and grasses.

A mirrorlike layer at the back of cats' eyes makes them glow when light shines on them.

Caring for cats

Many big cats are now endangered in the wild. Loss of habitat, hunting, and poaching are the main reasons for this. Game reserves and zoos play an important part in educating people, and in breeding and protecting rare species.

Two's company. . .
Most zoos and reserves in the world are part of an international breeding program. This ensures that the cats that are paired up are compatible, and can breed and produce healthy cubs.

Tourist attraction
Visits to game reserves are beneficial for both the cats and the tourists. Visitors get to see the animals in their natural environment, rather than in cages. The cats have lots of room to roam around. Visitors must be careful not to disturb the cats.

Lions can be bred in captivity very successfully.

DRIVE SLOWLY 40 KMH.
PLEASE STAY IN YOUR CAR.

EMBAKASI PLAINS
KAREN C.PRI.SCHOOL DAM 5 KM.
ELAND HOLLOW   7 KM.

8

LION P   3 KM.
ATHI   N CIRCUIT 5 KM.
HIPPO LS   8 KM.

MIDDLE RIDGE
MOKOYIET VALLEY   4 KM
SOSIAN VALLEY   4 KM

Saving the tiger

It is estimated that more than 400 tigers are killed each year, making them one of the most endangered big cats. Wildlife organizations set up safe, protected areas, called reserves, and install patrols to protect these cats.

A replacement mom

These young leopard cubs are being fed by a keeper. Cubs may be hand-reared in captivity if their mother dies or abandons them. If cubs are to be released into the wild at some stage, they will be handled as little as possible.

Adaptable cats

It is strange to see these lions in the snow, but their thick fur protects them from the cold. These animals were probably born in a protected environment and have never lived in the wild.

Glossary

Here are the meanings of some of the words
that are useful to know when learning about cats.

Ambush a surprise attack on prey.

Breeding when animals give birth
to young.

Broadleaf forest contains trees that
have broad flat leaves, and no needles
or cones.

Camouflage for cats, camouflage
is having fur that matches their
surroundings in color or pattern.
This is to avoid being seen by prey.

Carnivore an animal that eats the
flesh of another animal.

Coniferous forest contains trees that
produce cones, such as fir trees.

Feline relating to the cat family.

Flehmen cats have a special organ
in their mouths that allows
them to combine
taste and smell.

This process is known as the flehmen
response.

Fossil the preserved remains of a
creature or plant that was once alive.

Habitat the place where a creature
or plant naturally lives or grows.

Mammal a warm-blooded animal
with a hairy body and a backbone.
Female mammals produce milk to
feed their young.

Mane long hair that grows on
the neck and back of a lion.

Nocturnal active at night. Most cats
are nocturnal.

Predator an animal that hunts
other animals for food.

Prey an animal hunted for food.

Pride a group of lions.

Saber-toothed cats extinct members
of the cat family with long, curved
upper-canine teeth.

Solitary living alone.

Species a group of animals
or plants made up of related
individuals who are able to
produce young.

Stalking to approach prey quietly,
so that they do not notice until it is
too late.

Territory an area defended by an
animal, or animals, against others
of its kind.

Tropics the region between
the tropics of Cancer and Capricorn.
Many of the big cats live within
this area.

Tundra a cold, treeless area of the
Arctic Circle. Few animals live in
this environment.

Animal alphabet

Each cat featured in this book is listed here, along with its page number and some of its characteristics.

Bobcat 4, 37
A small North American lynx, with a short tail and a spotted reddish-brown coat.

Caracal 35
Found in the scrublands of Africa and Asia, this cat has tufted ears and can leap high into the air.

Cheetah 4, 7, 8, 22-23, 32
A spotted large cat, the cheetah is the fastest land animal on Earth. Found in east and central Africa, and a small area of Asia.

Clouded leopard 9, 25
A medium-sized cat with unusual, cloud-shaped markings and long canine teeth. It lives in southeastern Asia.

Domestic cat 4, 14-15
There are many different breeds of these small cats that are found throughout the world.

Fishing cat 37
A water-loving, medium-sized gray cat that has spots and stripes. It is found in southeastern Asia.

Jaguar 4, 6, 15, 20-21, 40-41
A powerful cat, the jaguar is found in Central and South America.

Leopard 4, 6, 10, 15, 24-25, 40, 43, 45
This tree-loving spotted cat is found in both Africa and Asia. Black leopards are called panthers.

Lion 4, 7, 9, 12, 15, 30-31, 38-39, 42, 44-45
    African 16-17
    Asiatic 17
The second biggest cat, and the only cat to live in groups called prides. Male lions have thick manes of hair.

Lynx 41
    European 36
    Spanish 35
A medium-sized cat with a short tail, spotted fur, and tufted ear-tips. There are many species of lynx in the world; some are very rare.

Ocelot 37
This spotted and striped medium-sized cat has a deep yellow or orange coat. It lives in Central and South America.

Panther 24
The name given to a black leopard, and occasionally to a black jaguar.

Puma 4-5, 6, 26-27, 33, 39
Pumas range from Canada, down through the US, to Central and South America. Other names given to the puma are cougar, mountain lion, and panther.

Serval 33, 34-35
This unusual long-legged, medium-sized cat is found in the grasslands of central, southern, and northwest Africa.

Smilodon 5
A saber-toothed cat that lived approximately 11,000 years ago.

Snow leopard 4, 7, 28-29
A large gray cat with spotted and blotchy markings. It lives in the mountains of central Asia.

Tiger, 4-5, 6-7, 15, 18-19, 39, 43, 45
    Amur 4, 18
    Bengal 18
The biggest of all the cats, there are several species of this powerful, striped feline.

Index

Acknowledgments

Dorling Kindersley would like to thank:
Beehive Illustrations (Andy Cooke) for original illustrations;
Andrew O'Brien for digital artwork p8; Sarah Mills for picture
library services; Anna Lofthouse and Samantha Gray for
editorial assistance; Chester Zoo; Philip Dowell.

Picture Credits:
The publisher would like to thank the following for their kind
permission to reproduce their photographs:
a=above; c=center; b=below; l=left; r=right; t=top;

Heather Angel: 15bl. Ardea London Ltd: John Daniels 44tr; Chris
Harvey 42c; Chuck McDougal 43b; Micheal Potland 45br. BBC Natural
History Unit: Peter Blackwell 30tl; Owen Newman 40-41c; Rico & Ruiz
35cl; Anup Shah 10b, 25c; Tom Vezo 41tr. Bruce Coleman Ltd: Trevor
Barrett 22tl; Bruce Coleman Inc 1c; Christer Fredriksson 24c; Hans
Reinhard 9tl; Pacific Stock 27tl. Corbis: Yann Arthus-Bertrand 30-31c;
Gallo Images 34-35c; Mary Ann MacDonald 35r. Ecoscene: S.K Tiwari

45t. FLPA - Images of nature: R Bender 36c; C Elsey 31br; David
Hosking 3r; Gerard Lacz 15tr, 20tr; Leonard Lee Rue 17tc; Jurgen and
Christine Sohns 21tr; Terry Whittaker 28tr. ImageState: 11t, 22-23;
National Geographic 11b. N.H.P.A.: Martin Harvey 25tr, 45cl; T.
Kitchin & V. Hurst 7c, 14c, 28-29c; E.A Janes 39tr; Rich Kirchner 29br;
Gerald Lacz 7tl; Christophe Ratier 32c; Andy Rouse 18bl, 19c, 20-21c;
25bc, 26-27c; Kevin Schafer 23tr; Jonathan and Angela Scott 38-39c;
Ann and Steve Toon 16-17c. Oxford Scientific Films: Ken Cole 41tl;
Judd Cooney 27tr; Clyde Lockwood 33r; Stan Osolinski 44b; Maurice
Tibbles 12bl; Steve Turner 7br, 46l, 47r; Konrad Wothe 18tr; Belinda
Wright 37tl. Science Photo Library: William Ervin 39tl, 43t. Still
Pictures: Brunner-Unep 23bc; Roland Seitre 12-13c. Telegraph Colour
Library: Richard Matthews 33tl.

Jacket images: Bruce Coleman Ltd: Joe McDonald br. Gettyone
stone:Tim Davis t. N.H.P.A.: Andy Rouse bl; Kevin Schafer bc.
Oxford Scientific Films: Richard Packwood back cover.

All other images: © Dorling Kindersley. For further information,
see www.dkimages.com